NANCY TUMINELLY

Cool NUT-FREE RECIPES

DELICIOUS & FUN FOODS WITHOUT NUTS

A Division of ABDO
ABDO
Publishing Company

visit us at www.abdopublishing.com

Published by ABDO Publishing Company, a division of ABDO, P.O. Box 398166, Minneapolis, Minnesota 55439. Copyright © 2013 by Abdo Consulting Group, Inc. International copyrights reserved in all countries. No part of this book may be reproduced in any form without written permission from the publisher. Checkerboard Library™ is a trademark and logo of ABDO Publishing Company.

Printed in the United States of America, North Mankato, Minnesota
102012
012013

♻ PRINTED ON RECYCLED PAPER

Design and Production: Mighty Media, Inc.
Series Editor: Liz Salzmann
Photo Credits: Aaron DeYoe, Shutterstock

The following manufacturers/names appearing in this book are trademarks: Pyrex®, Kitchen Aid®, Roundy's®, La Preferida®, Kraft®, Hellman's®, Pillsbury®, Hidden Valley®, Enjoy Life®, Ultra Grain®, Proctor-Silex®

Library of Congress Cataloging-in-Publication Data

Tuminelly, Nancy, 1952-
  Cool nut-free recipes : delicious & fun foods without nuts / Nancy Tuminelly.
    pages cm. -- (Cool recipes for your health)
  Audience: 8-12
  Includes bibliographical references and index.
  ISBN 978-1-61783-583-4
  1. Cooking--Juvenile literature. 2. Nut-free diet--Recipes--Juvenile literature.
  I. Title.
  TX652.5.T8423 2013
  641.5'6318--dc23
                              2012023999

TO ADULT HELPERS

This is your chance to introduce newcomers to the fun of cooking! As children learn to cook, they develop new skills, gain confidence, and make some delicious food.

These recipes are designed to help children cook fun and healthy dishes. They may need more adult assistance for some recipes than others. Be there to offer help and guidance when needed, but encourage them to do as much as they can on their own. Also encourage them to be creative by using the variations listed or trying their own ideas. Building creativity into the cooking process encourages children to think like real chefs.

Before getting started, establish rules for using the kitchen, cooking tools, and ingredients. It is important for children to have adult supervision when using sharp tools, the oven, or the stove.

Most of all, be there to cheer on your new chefs. Put on your apron and stand by. Watch and learn. Taste their creations. Praise their efforts. Enjoy the culinary adventure!

CONTENTS

NUT-FREE

Read the ingredients listed on any food package.
If it says "Made in a factory that also processes nuts" or
"May contain nuts" don't use it!

LEARN MORE ABOUT COOKING NUT-FREE MEALS!

Following a nut-free diet means that you don't eat anything made with nuts. Some people don't eat nuts because they don't like the taste. Other people are allergic to nuts. Nut allergies can be very serious. Some people need immediate **medical** help if they accidentally eat nuts.

There are a lot of foods for people who don't eat nuts. Try some of the nut-free recipes in this book!

When shopping, look for fresh ingredients. Be sure to avoid things that might be made with nuts. Read the labels carefully.

Sometimes a recipe that includes nuts will list nut-free **options** for those ingredients. Or, be creative and make up your own **variations**. Being a chef is all about using your imagination.

SAFETY FIRST!

Some recipes call for activities or ingredients that require caution. If you see these symbols, ask an adult for help!

Hot - This recipe requires handling hot objects. Always use oven mitts when holding hot pans.

Sharp - You need to use a sharp knife or cutting tool for this recipe. Ask an adult to help out.

THE BASICS

ASK PERMISSION

Before you cook, ask **permission** to use the kitchen, cooking tools, and ingredients. If you'd like to do something yourself, say so! If you would like help, ask for it!

BE NEAT AND CLEAN

- Start with clean hands, clean tools, and a clean work surface.
- Wear comfortable clothing.
- Tie back long hair and roll up your sleeves so they stay out of the food.

NO GERMS ALLOWED!

Raw eggs and raw meat have bacteria in them that can make you sick. After you handle raw eggs or meat, wash your hands, tools, and work surfaces with soap and water. Keep everything clean!

BE PREPARED

- Be organized. Knowing where everything is makes cooking easier!
- Read the directions all the way through before you start cooking.
- Set out all your ingredients before starting.

BE SMART, BE SAFE

- Never work alone in the kitchen.
- Ask an adult before using anything hot or sharp, such as a stove top, oven, knife, or **grater**.
- Turn pot handles toward the back of the stove to avoid accidentally knocking them over.

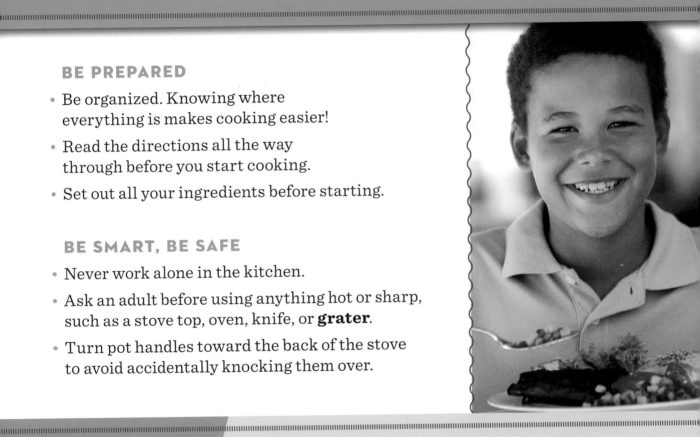

MEASURING

Many ingredients are measured by the cup, tablespoon, or teaspoon. Some ingredients are measured by weight in ounces or pounds. You can buy food by its weight too.

THE TOOL BOX

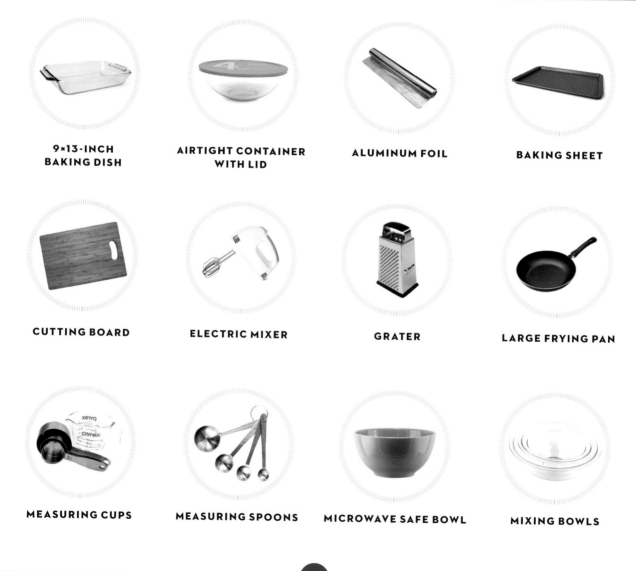

9×13-INCH BAKING DISH

AIRTIGHT CONTAINER WITH LID

ALUMINUM FOIL

BAKING SHEET

CUTTING BOARD

ELECTRIC MIXER

GRATER

LARGE FRYING PAN

MEASURING CUPS

MEASURING SPOONS

MICROWAVE SAFE BOWL

MIXING BOWLS

The tools you will need for the recipes in this book are listed below. When a recipe says to use a tool you don't recognize, turn back to these pages to see what it looks like.

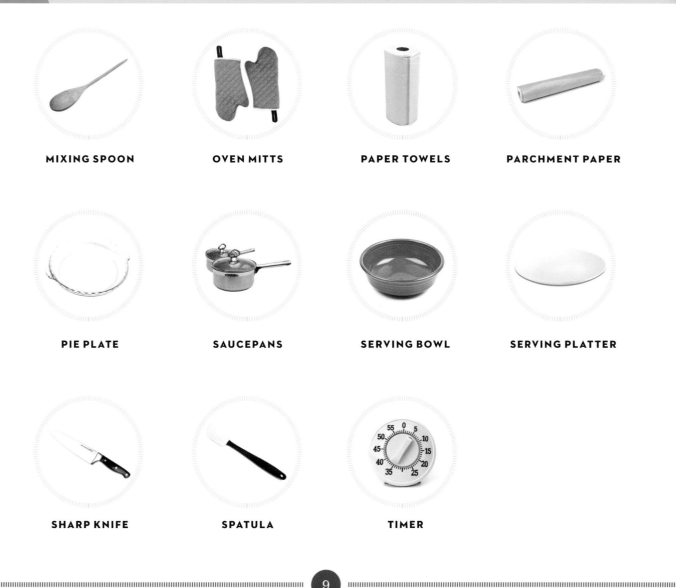

MIXING SPOON

OVEN MITTS

PAPER TOWELS

PARCHMENT PAPER

PIE PLATE

SAUCEPANS

SERVING BOWL

SERVING PLATTER

SHARP KNIFE

SPATULA

TIMER

COOL INGREDIENTS

12-INCH FLOUR TORTILLAS

BLACK OLIVES

BROWN SUGAR

CANNED BEANS (KIDNEY & PINTO)

CANNED CRANBERRY SAUCE

CANNED TOMATOES IN GARLIC WATER

CATALINA DRESSING

CELERY

CHEESE (CHEDDAR, CREAM CHEESE)

CHICKEN BREASTS

DRIED FRUIT (BLUEBERRIES, CHERRIES, APRICOTS)

FRUIT (APPLES & PEARS)

GOLDEN RAISINS

LEMON JUICE

MAYONNAISE

MILK CHOCOLATE CHIPS

Many of these recipes call for basic ingredients such as salt, non-stick cooking spray, butter, eggs, olive oil, and baking soda. Here are other ingredients needed for the recipes in this book.

NUT-FREE GRANOLA

ONION SOUP MIX

ONIONS (WHITE AND GREEN)

POTATO CHIPS

PRE-MADE PIE CRUST

PRETZELS

RANCH DRESSING MIX

RED BELL PEPPER

ROLLED OATS

SEMI-SWEET CHOCOLATE CHIPS

SPICES (SMOKED PAPRIKA, GROUND CINNAMON)

SUNFLOWER SEEDS

TOFFEE BITS

VANILLA EXTRACT

WHEAT GERM

WHOLE WHEAT FLOUR

COOKING TERMS

ARRANGE

Arrange means to place things in a certain order or pattern.

BEAT

Beat means to mix well using a whisk or electric mixer.

CHOP

Chop means to cut into small pieces.

DICE

Dice means to cut something into really small pieces with a knife.

DRAIN

Drain means to remove liquid using a strainer or colander.

Always wash fruit and vegetables well. Rinse them under cold water.
Pat them dry with a **towel**. Then they won't slip when you cut them.

GRATE

Grate means to shred something into small pieces using a **grater**.

ROLL

Roll means to wrap something around itself into a tube.

SLICE

Slice means to cut food into pieces of the same thickness.

SPREAD

Spread means to make an even layer with a spoon, knife, or spatula.

STIR

Stir means to mix ingredients together, usually with a large spoon.

CHEESE & APPLE DIP

makes 2 cups

INGREDIENTS

8 ounces cream cheese, softened

½ cup mayonnaise

½ cup cheddar cheese, grated

½ cup apples, finely chopped

potato chips

TOOLS

measuring cups & spoons

large mixing bowl

electric mixer

grater

sharp knife

cutting board

mixing spoon

serving bowl

serving platter

1. Put the cream cheese and mayonnaise in a mixing bowl. Beat with an electric mixer until smooth.

2. Add the cheddar cheese and apples.

3. Stir until all of the ingredients are combined.

4. Put the dip in a serving bowl. Place it on a serving platter. Surround the bowl with potato chips for dipping.

EVEN COOLER!

Instead of chips, try using pretzels, bread sticks, carrots, celery, broccoli, or cucumber.

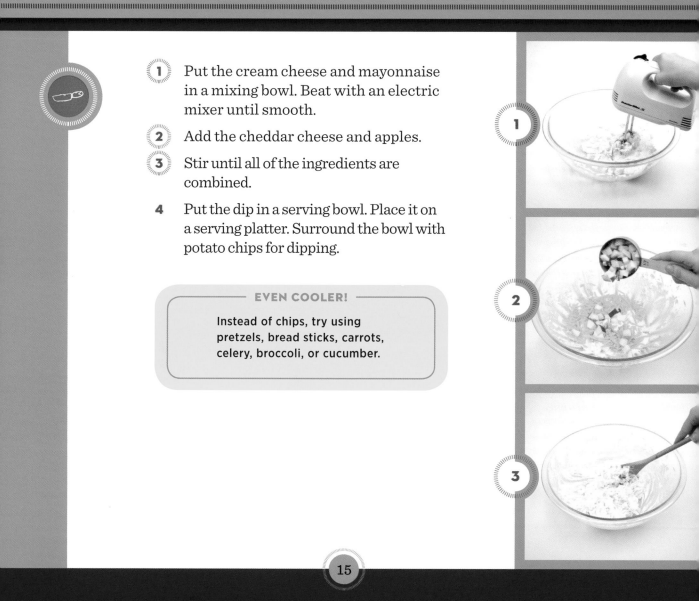

BEAN GOULASH

makes 4 servings

INGREDIENTS

1 tablespoon olive oil

1 large onion, finely chopped

1 tablespoon smoked paprika

14-ounce can diced tomatoes with garlic

8-ounce can kidney beans, drained

8-ounce can pinto beans, drained

TOOLS

measuring cups & spoons

large frying pan

sharp knife

cutting board

mixing spoon

timer

A NEW TWIST ON A CLASSIC HUNGARIAN DISH!

1. Heat the oil in a frying pan over medium-high heat. Add the onion and cook for 5 minutes. Stir well.

2. Stir in the paprika. Cook for 1 minute.

3. Stir in the tomatoes. Fill the empty can half full of water. Add the water to the onion mixture. Cook for 10 minutes.

4. Add the kidney and pinto beans. Cook for 2 minutes. Remember to stir!

5. Serve the goulash with slices of bread.

EVEN COOLER!

Try topping the goulash with parsley, sour cream, or grated cheese!

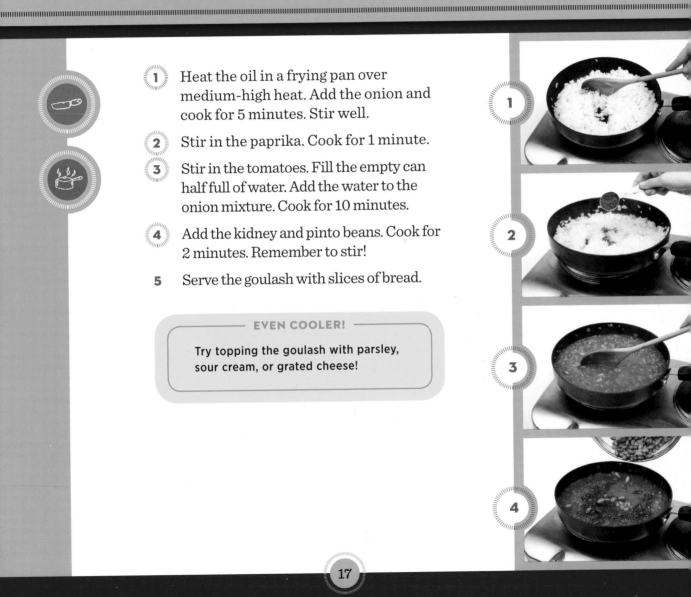

SIMPLE SNACK MIXERS

makes 2 cups

INGREDIENTS

½ cup sunflower seeds

½ cup golden raisins

½ cup nut-free granola

½ cup dried cherries

¼ cup dried apricots, chopped

TOOLS

measuring cups

large airtight container

serving bowl

sharp knife

cutting board

1. Put all the ingredients in a container with a lid. Seal the lid tightly.

2. Shake the container to mix the ingredients.

3. Put some out in a serving bowl for your friends.

EVEN COOLER!

Try adding ½ cup of chocolate chips for a sweeter treat! If you want more fruit, try dried bananas or dried pineapple!

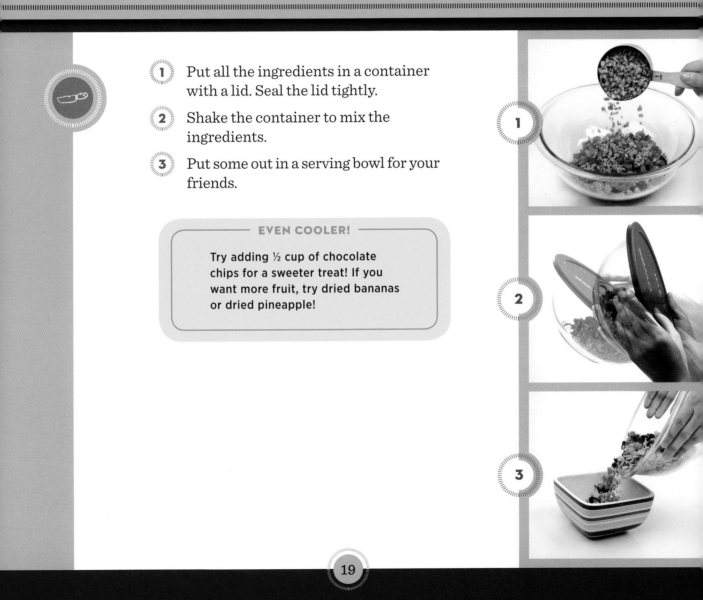

CRANBERRY CHICKEN

makes 6 servings

INGREDIENTS

non-stick cooking spray

6 chicken breast halves

16-ounce bottle of Catalina dressing

1-ounce envelope of dry onion soup mix

16-ounce can cranberry sauce with berries

TOOLS

9×13-inch baking dish

cutting board

paper towels

large mixing bowl

mixing spoon

oven mitts

timer

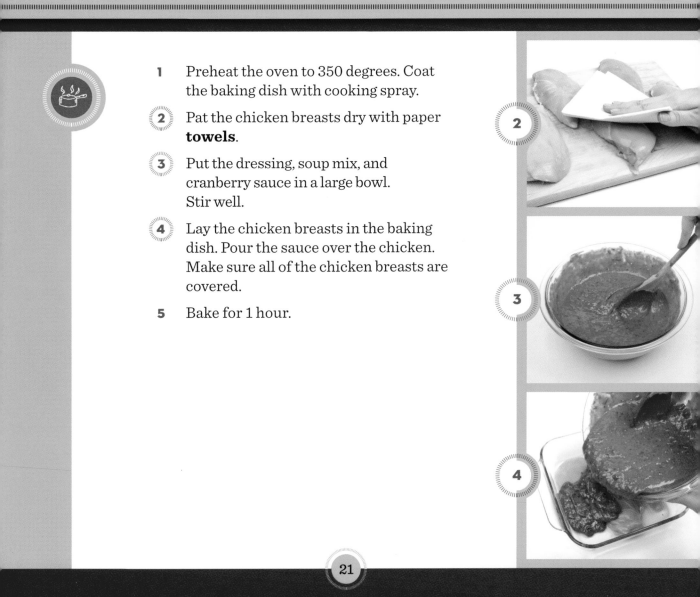

1. Preheat the oven to 350 degrees. Coat the baking dish with cooking spray.

2. Pat the chicken breasts dry with paper **towels**.

3. Put the dressing, soup mix, and cranberry sauce in a large bowl. Stir well.

4. Lay the chicken breasts in the baking dish. Pour the sauce over the chicken. Make sure all of the chicken breasts are covered.

5. Bake for 1 hour.

PARTY PINWHEELS

makes 10 servings

INGREDIENTS

16 ounces cream cheese, softened

1-ounce package ranch dressing mix

2 green onions, chopped

4 12-inch flour tortillas

½ cup red bell pepper, diced

½ cup celery, diced

2-ounce can sliced black olives

½ cup cheddar cheese, grated

TOOLS

sharp knife

cutting board

medium mixing bowl

electric mixer

measuring cups & spoons

grater

aluminum foil

22

1   Put the cream cheese, dressing mix, and green onions in a mixing bowl. Beat together with an electric mixer.

2   Lay a tortilla on a cutting board.

3   Spread one-fourth of the cream cheese mixture on the tortilla. Put one-fourth of the red pepper, celery, olives and cheese on top.

4   Roll up the tortilla. Then wrap it in aluminum foil.

5   Repeat steps 2 through 4 with the remaining tortillas.

6   Put the rolls in the refrigerator for 2 hours.

7   Take off the foil. Cut the ends off the rolls and **discard** them. Slice the rolls into 1-inch sections.

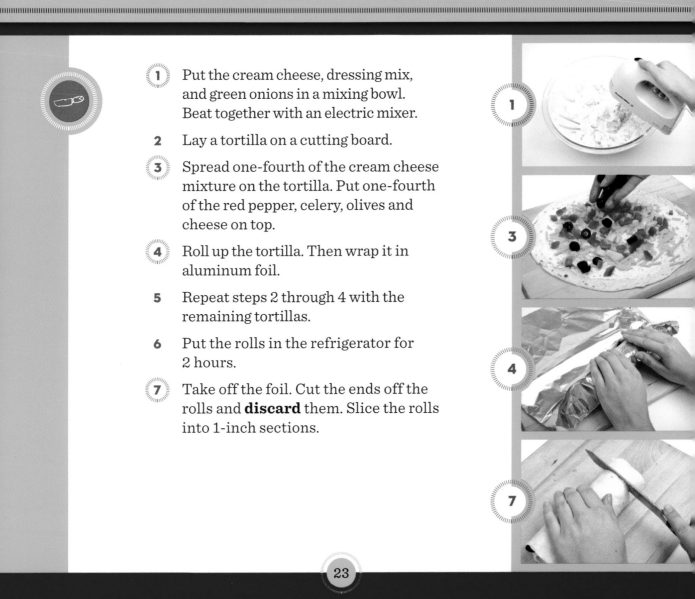

CHOCOLATE BARK

makes 18 servings

INGREDIENTS

1 cup milk
chocolate chips

1½ cups semi-sweet
chocolate chips

2 cups pretzels,
broken into pieces

1 cup nut-free
toffee bits

TOOLS

measuring cups

large microwave-
safe bowl

mixing spoon

baking sheet

parchment paper

spatula

1   Put the chocolate chips in a microwave-safe bowl. Microwave on high for 10 seconds. Stir and then microwave for 10 more seconds. Continue to cook 10 seconds at a time until the chocolate is melted.

2   Stir in the pretzel pieces and nut-free toffee bits.

3   Line the baking sheet with parchment paper. Spread the mixture evenly on the baking sheet.

4   Put the baking sheet in the freezer. Freeze for 1 hour.

5   Remove it from the freezer. Break the bark into pieces with your hands.

6   Put the pieces in the refrigerator for 1 hour or until ready to serve.

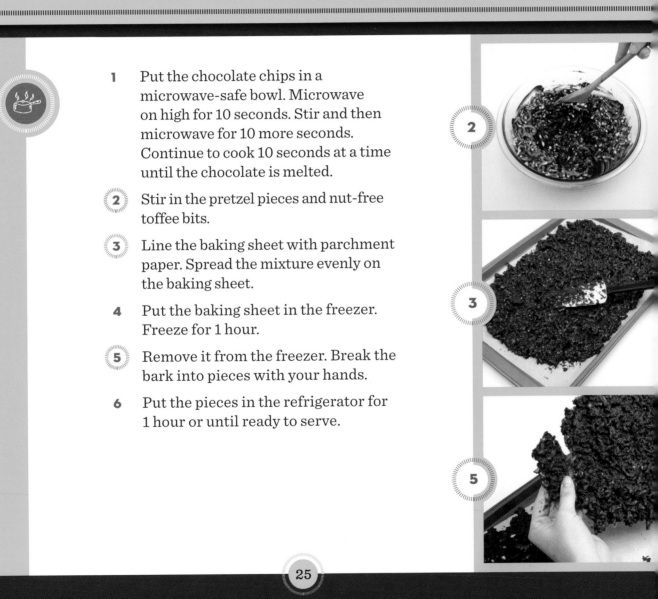

25

MIXED FRUIT PIE

makes 8 servings

INGREDIENTS

non-stick cooking spray

1 pre-made pie crust

1 pear, diced

1 apple, diced

4 tablespoons brown sugar

1½ teaspoons vanilla extract

2 tablespoons lemon juice

¼ teaspoon salt

¼ cup dried blueberries

TOOLS

pie plate

sharp knife

cutting board

measuring cups & spoons

large saucepan

mixing spoon

oven mitts

timer

1. Preheat the oven to 350 degrees. Coat the pie plate with cooking spray.

2. Press the pre-made pie crust into the pie plate.

3. Bake for 25 minutes, or until golden brown. Remove the pie plate from the oven. Set aside to cool.

4. Heat the pear, apple, brown sugar, vanilla, lemon juice, and salt in a large saucepan over low heat. Stir often. Cook for 30 to 40 minutes, or until the fruit is soft. Add the blueberries. Cook for 5 more minutes. Remove saucepan from heat. Let it cool.

5. Pour the cooled fruit mixture into the cooled crust.

6. Sprinkle some brown sugar on top and bake for 25 minutes. Remove it from the oven. Let it cool before serving.

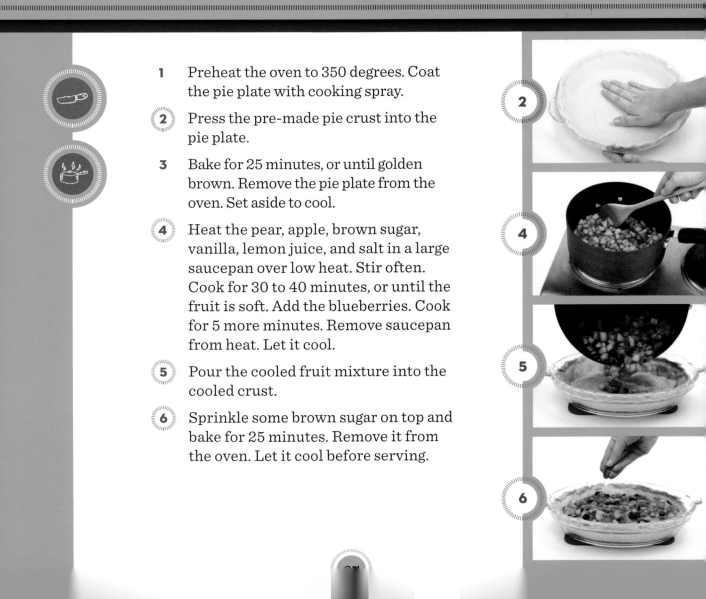

OATMEAL COOKIES

makes 24 cookies

INGREDIENTS

1 cup butter, softened

1½ cups brown sugar

2 eggs

½ teaspoon vanilla extract

1½ cups whole wheat flour

1 teaspoon baking soda

1 teaspoon salt

½ teaspoon ground cinnamon

2 cups nut-free rolled oats

½ cup wheat germ

TOOLS

measuring cups & spoons

2 mixing bowls

electric mixer

mixing spoon

aluminum foil

sharp knife

cutting board

baking sheet

oven mitts

timer

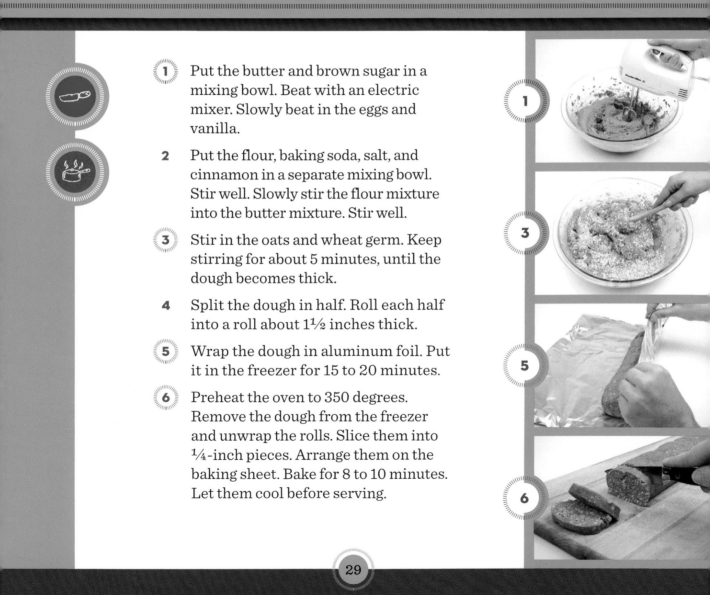

1. Put the butter and brown sugar in a mixing bowl. Beat with an electric mixer. Slowly beat in the eggs and vanilla.

2. Put the flour, baking soda, salt, and cinnamon in a separate mixing bowl. Stir well. Slowly stir the flour mixture into the butter mixture. Stir well.

3. Stir in the oats and wheat germ. Keep stirring for about 5 minutes, until the dough becomes thick.

4. Split the dough in half. Roll each half into a roll about 1½ inches thick.

5. Wrap the dough in aluminum foil. Put it in the freezer for 15 to 20 minutes.

6. Preheat the oven to 350 degrees. Remove the dough from the freezer and unwrap the rolls. Slice them into ¼-inch pieces. Arrange them on the baking sheet. Bake for 8 to 10 minutes. Let them cool before serving.

more about NUT-FREE LIFE

If you liked these dishes, look for other nut-free foods. If you want or need to avoid eating nuts, you have a lot of **options**!

Many people like to snack on nuts. Keep your kitchen stocked with healthy, nut-free **alternatives**, such as fresh fruits or vegetables. Some great nut substitutes to try include sunflower seeds, pumpkin seeds, rolled oats, and crisp rice cereal.

Now you're ready to start making your own nut-free recipes. It takes creativity and planning. Check out different cookbooks. Look through the lists of ingredients. You'll be surprised how many dishes don't need nuts. Or you can come up with your own recipes or **variations**. The kitchen is calling!

If you have a nut allergy, cooking meals at home is safer than eating out. Sometimes restaurants can accidentally put nuts in your food.

GLOSSARY

ALTERNATIVE - something you can choose instead.

DISCARD - to throw away.

GRATER - a tool with rough-edged holes used to shred something into small pieces.

MEDICAL - having to do with doctors or the science of medicine.

OPTION - something you can choose.

PERMISSION - when a person in charge says it's okay to do something.

TOWEL - a cloth or paper used for cleaning or drying.

VARIATION - a change in form, position, or condition.

WEB SITES

To learn more about cooking for your health, visit ABDO Publishing Company on the Internet at www.abdopublishing.com. Web sites about creative ways for kids to cook healthy food are featured on our Book Links page. These links are routinely monitored and updated to provide the most current information available.

INDEX